The · Life Cycle · Series

The Life Cycle of a

Crayfish

Bobbie Kalman & Rebecca Sjonger

Crabtree Publishing Company

www.crabtreebooks.com

The Life Cycle Series
A Bobbie Kalman Book
Dedicated by Ken Wright
To Frenchie & Zack, "Good friends"

Editor-in-Chief
Bobbie Kalman

Writing team
Bobbie Kalman
Rebecca Sjonger

Substantive editor
Kathryn Smithyman

Project editor
Michael Hodge

Editors
Molly Aloian
Robin Johnson
Kelley MacAulay

Design
Margaret Amy Salter

Production coordinator
Heather Fitzpatrick

Photo research
Crystal Foxton

Consultant
Patricia Loesche, Ph.D., Animal Behavior Program, Department of Psychology, University of Washington

Special thanks to
Jeff Cook and Koen Breedveld of Spring Rivers Foundation (springrivers.org), Dustin Saumier, and Devin Saumier

Illustrations
Barbara Bedell: pages 5 (shrimp), 18 (plankton)
Bonna Rouse: back cover, pages 4, 7, 10-11, 13, 14, 15, 17, 18 (crayfish)
Margaret Amy Salter: pages 5 (crab and lobster), 18 (magnifying glass)

Photographs
Animals Animals - Earth Scenes: © Nelson, Alan G.: page 26; © OSF/Brown, R.: page 5
Andrew Dennis/ANTPhoto.com: page 17
AP/Wide World Photos: page 29 (bottom)
Bruce Coleman Inc.: Danial J. Lyons: pages 14, 20; Leonard Rue Jr.: page 23 (top)
Marc Crabtree: page 30
Katherine Kantor: title page, page 31 (bottom)
© Dwight Kuhn: pages 4, 12 (bottom), 16, 24-25
marinethemes.com/Kelvin Aitken: pages 12 (top), 27
© Barry Mansell/naturepl.com: page 23 (bottom)
A.N.T. Photo Library/NHPA: page 6
Photo Researchers, Inc.: Gary Meszaros: pages 8-9; Mark Smith: front cover
Spring Rivers Foundation: Koen Breedveld: pages 3, 11, 28 (top), 29 (top); Jeff Cook: page 31 (top)
Visuals Unlimited: Bill Beatty: pages 19, 22; Gary Meszaros: page 21; Doug Sizemore: page 15
Other images by Photodisc

Library and Archives Canada Cataloguing in Publication

Kalman, Bobbie, date.
The life cycle of a crayfish / Bobbie Kalman & Rebecca Sjonger.

(The Life cycle series)
Includes index.
ISBN-13: 978-0-7787-0629-8 (bound)
ISBN-13: 978-0-7787-0703-5 (pbk.)
ISBN-10: 0-7787-0629-X (bound)
ISBN-10: 0-7787-0703-2 (pbk.)
1. Crayfish--Life cycles--Juvenile literature. I. Sjonger, Rebecca
II. Title. III. Series.

QL444.M33K34 2006   j595.3'84   C2006-904126-1

Library of Congress Cataloging-in-Publication Data

Kalman, Bobbie.
The life cycle of a crayfish / Bobbie Kalman & Rebecca Sjonger.
p. cm. -- (The life cycle series)
ISBN-13: 978-0-7787-0629-8 (rlb)
ISBN-10: 0-7787-0629-X (rlb)
ISBN-13: 978-0-7787-0703-5 (pb)
ISBN-10: 0-7787-0703-2 (pb)
1. Crayfish--Life cycles--Juvenile literature. I. Sjonger, Rebecca. II. Title.
III. Series.

QL444.M33K345 2007
595.3'84--dc22
                    2006023370

Crabtree Publishing Company

www.crabtreebooks.com   1-800-387-7650

Published in Canada
Crabtree Publishing
616 Welland Ave.
St. Catharines, ON
L2M 5V6

Published in the United States
Crabtree Publishing
PMB16A
350 Fifth Ave., Suite 3308
New York, NY 10118

Published in the United Kingdom
Crabtree Publishing
White Cross Mills
High Town, Lancaster
LA1 4XS

Published in Australia
Crabtree Publishing
386 Mt. Alexander Rd.
Ascot Vale (Melbourne)
VIC 3032

Contents

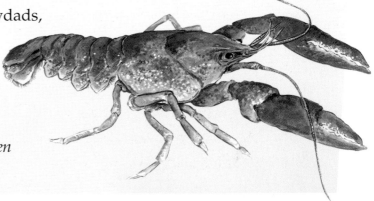

What are crayfish?

Crayfish are animals called **crustaceans**. Crustaceans are **arthropods** that live mainly in water. Arthropods are animals with bodies that are made up of many **segments**, or small parts. The segments are joined together.

Like all arthropods, crayfish do not have backbones. Instead of backbones, crayfish have **exoskeletons**. Exoskeletons are hard coverings on the bodies of crayfish. Exoskeletons are made of a tough material called **chitin**.

A crayfish by any other name

People from different places have different names for crayfish. Crayfish are also known as crawdads, crawfish, freshwater lobsters, mudbugs, and spoondogs. Crustaceans called sea crayfish are not actually crayfish, however. Sea crayfish are really lobsters!

In the southwestern United States, crayfish are often called crawdads.

Cool crays

Crayfish are **cold-blooded** animals. The body temperature of a cold-blooded animal changes as the temperature of the air or water around the animal changes. Most crayfish live in water. Crayfish breathe under water using body parts called **gills**.

This Lamington spiny crayfish lives in streams in Australia.

Crayfish relatives

Crayfish are related to other crustaceans, including shrimp, crabs, and lobsters. Some crayfish look a lot like some lobsters. The bodies of lobsters are usually much larger than the bodies of crayfish are, however. Most crayfish live in **fresh water**, whereas most lobsters live in **salt water**. Fresh water contains very little salt. Lakes and rivers have fresh water. Salt water contains a lot of salt. Seas and oceans have salt water.

shrimp

crab

lobster

So many species!

There are over 540 **species**, or types, of crayfish. Scientists do not know exactly how many crayfish species there are. Every year, scientists discover new species! Different crayfish species live in different parts of the world. About 350 species of crayfish live in North America. Over 100 crayfish species live in Australia. The remaining species live in other **continents** around the world.

Australian crayfish, such as this yabby, are often larger than North American crayfish are.

A lot of looks

Different crayfish species are different colors and sizes. Crayfish may be black, blue, brown, green, pink, red, white, or yellow. Some species have **multicolored** bodies. Many crayfish are about three inches (8 cm) long, but some grow to be over sixteen inches (41 cm) long. Some common crayfish species are shown on this page.

swamp crayfish

white-clawed crayfish

red swamp crayfish

Tasmanian giant crayfish

Crayfish habitats

Crayfish live on every continent except Africa and Antarctica. The **climate** in Africa is too hot for crayfish to survive, and the climate in Antarctica is too cold for crayfish to survive. Climate is the long-term weather conditions in an area. Most crayfish live in **temperate** areas of the world. In temperate areas, the weather changes as the seasons change. Many temperate areas do not become extremely hot or extremely cold.

Freshwater habitats

The natural place where an animal lives is called its **habitat**. Freshwater rivers, lakes, streams, swamps, and ponds are crayfish habitats. Crayfish usually live on the bottoms of shallow bodies of water, where there is plenty of food. They spend time among underwater plants, between rocks, or in soil. The waters in which crayfish live may become icy in winter, but they never freeze completely.

This red swamp crayfish lives at the bottom of a river.

A crayfish's body

A crayfish's body has two main sections—a **cephalothorax** and an **abdomen**. The cephalothorax is made up of the crayfish's head and its **thorax**, or midsection. The head and thorax are joined together. The cephalothorax contains the crayfish's **organs**. The abdomen is the crayfish's rear body section. It is sometimes called a tail.

*The **carapace** is part of the crayfish's exoskeleton. It covers the soft cephalothorax and gills.*

*A crayfish has two **compound eyes**.*

*A crayfish touches, smells, and tastes with one long pair of **antennae** and one short pair of antennae.*

chelipeds

Ten legs

A crayfish has ten legs attached to its cephalothorax. The front two legs, called **chelipeds**, are larger than the other legs are. The chelipeds have claws on the ends. A crayfish uses them to push food into its mouth and to defend itself from **predators**. Predators are animals that hunt other animals for food. The crayfish uses its other eight legs to walk.

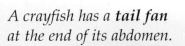

*A crayfish has a **tail fan** at the end of its abdomen.*

*The crayfish uses its **swimmerets** mainly to help it swim. The swimmerets are on the bottom of the crayfish's abdomen.*

cephalothorax

abdomen

walking legs

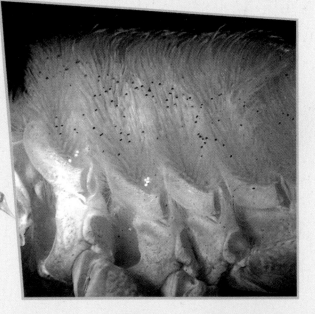

How a crayfish's gills work

A crayfish has nine sets of gills. There is a set of gills at the top of each walking leg. These gills are under the carapace. There is also a set of gills in the crayfish's mouth. The gills take in **oxygen** from water and send it through the crayfish's body. Oxygen is a gas in air and water that all animals breathe.

What is a life cycle?

This crayfish is an adult.
It can mate and have babies of its own.

A **life cycle** is a set of changes in an animal's life as its body develops. Near the beginning of its life cycle, a baby animal is born or hatches from an egg. The young animal grows and changes until it becomes an adult. An adult animal can **mate**. To mate is to join together with another animal of the same species to make babies.

Life spans

A life cycle is not the same as a **life span**. A life span is the length of time that an animal is alive. Different species of crayfish have different life spans. Crayfish live from two to twenty years. Large crayfish live longer than smaller crayfish do. The oldest known crayfish lived to be at least 30 years old!

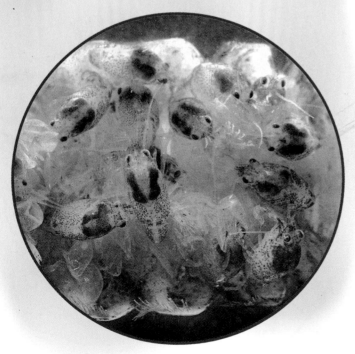

Young crayfish look like small adult crayfish.

A crayfish's life cycle

A crayfish begins its life cycle as an **embryo**, or developing animal. The embryo is inside an egg laid by its mother. When the crayfish hatches from the egg, it is called a **first instar**. The first instar stays with its mother. Soon, it **molts**, or sheds, its exoskeleton and grows a new exoskeleton. After it molts, the young crayfish is known as a **second instar**.

The second instar continues to live with its mother. After molting a second time, the crayfish is a **third instar**. At this stage in its life cycle, the crayfish leaves its mother and lives on its own. The crayfish keeps growing and molting until it becomes an adult. The adult crayfish can mate. After mating, female crayfish lay eggs. A new life cycle begins with each egg.

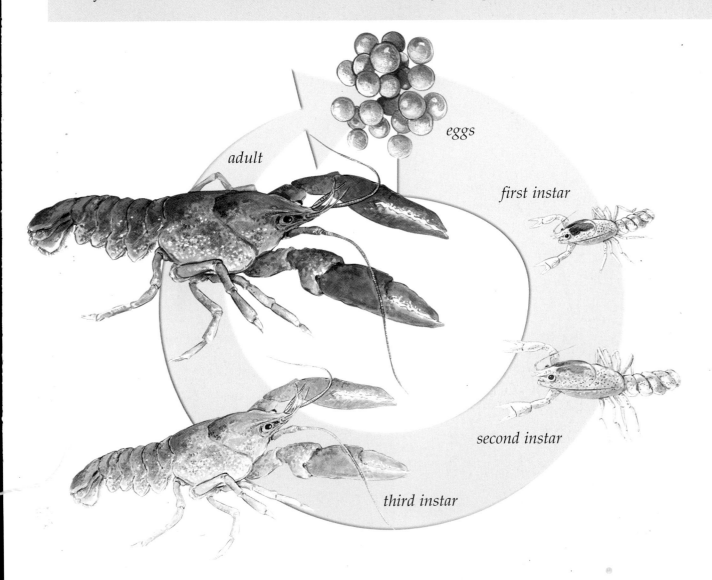

adult

eggs

first instar

second instar

third instar

Eggs on Mom

Most female crustaceans release their eggs into the water and do not care for them. A female crayfish carries her eggs on her swimmerets, however. Before laying her eggs, she makes a sticky substance in her body. She then spreads the substance onto her swimmerets to hold the eggs in place. By carrying her eggs, a female crayfish protects them from predators.

A large female crayfish may carry hundreds of eggs, whereas a smaller female may carry only dozens of eggs.

Inside the egg

Inside its egg, a crayfish embryo develops swimmerets, legs, and other body parts. The length of time an embryo needs to develop depends on its species. The embryos of some species need two weeks to develop. The embryos of other species take up to twenty weeks to develop. The length of time the embryo needs to develop inside its egg also depends on the temperature of the water in which the mother lives.

Embryos develop faster in warm water than they do in cool water. Embryos get the **energy** they need to grow from **yolk**, or liquid food. The yolk is in a **yolk sac**. The yolk sac is inside the embryo's body.

Egg groomer

A mother crayfish **grooms** her eggs by swishing water around her swimmerets. Grooming the eggs keeps them clean. It also helps oxygen from the water flow through the eggs to the growing embryos inside.

Not all crayfish eggs are the same size. The eggs of large crayfish are bigger than the eggs of small crayfish are.

First and second instars

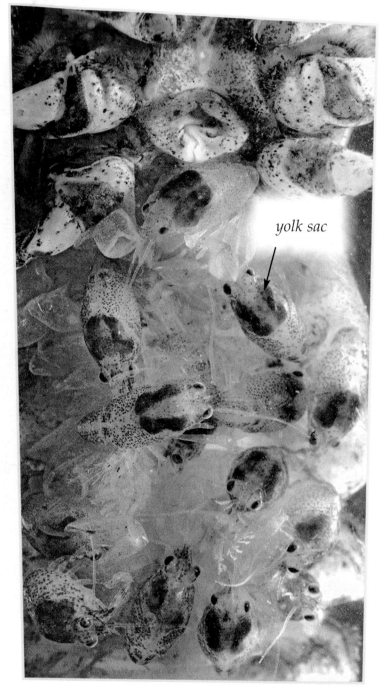

You can see the yolk sacs of these first instars through their carapaces.

yolk sac

When first instars wriggle out of their eggs, their bodies are still stuck to their mother's swimmerets. The mother crayfish grooms the first instars to keep water flowing over their bodies, just as she groomed her eggs. The first instars need to get oxygen from water in order to breathe.

Adult look-alikes

A first instar has the same body parts as those of an adult crayfish. The first instar is tiny and weak, however. Its body is **transparent**, or see-through. The first instar continues to get energy from its yolk. The yolk contains the **nutrients** the first instar needs to continue growing.

I'm molting!

The first instar's body continues to grow, but its exoskeleton does not grow. The first instar must molt when its exoskeleton becomes too tight. A new soft exoskeleton forms underneath the old tight one. The old exoskeleton cracks open and soon falls off. The crayfish is now a second instar.

Hold on!

During its molt, the second instar becomes unstuck from its mother's body. It uses its chelipeds to hold on to its mother's swimmerets.

Second instar

After molting, the second instar takes in water through its gills. Taking in water makes its body swell. The new exoskeleton slowly hardens over the second instar's swollen body. When its new exoskeleton is hard, the second instar releases the water from its body to make room to grow in its new exoskeleton! The second instar continues to get energy from its yolk as it grows larger.

Crayfish instars are not very active while they are attached to their mother.

On its own

By the time the second instar has used up its yolk, its body has grown too big for its exoskeleton. It molts and becomes a third instar. The third instar leaves its mother to live on its own for the rest of its life. It starts looking for food. It eats mainly **plankton**. Plankton is made up of tiny plants and animals that float in water.

plankton

Third instars

Third instars grow quickly! They must molt after a few weeks. Some small crayfish species become adults after this molt. Larger crayfish that have longer life spans are not yet fully grown. They continue to grow slowly over several years. Large crayfish species must molt more times before they become adults.

Molting and growing

Crayfish face many dangers while they molt. Molting crayfish cannot move to find food or to avoid predators. Before they molt, crayfish eat a lot of food. They then find places to molt where predators are not likely to notice them. After molting, some crayfish eat their old exoskeletons. The exoskeletons contain nutrients. The nutrients help the new exoskeleton harden.

exoskeleton

crayfish

Slow growing

Crayfish grow more slowly as they get older. As a result, the time between molts is longer for older crayfish than it is for younger crayfish. Adult crayfish molt about once a year.

This crayfish has just finished molting. Its old exoskeleton is on its left.

Mating

Adult crayfish are able to mate. Most crayfish mate in early spring. A male crayfish uses his senses of smell and sight to find a female crayfish. Once the male finds a female, he holds her and releases **sperm** into her body.

Sperm is a liquid that **fertilizes** eggs. The female crayfish stores the sperm inside her body. She leaves the male and finds a safe spot in which to lay her eggs.

An adult crayfish usually mates only two or three times during its lifetime.

Laying eggs

When a female crayfish is ready to lay eggs, she moves her swimmerets over her abdomen to clean it. She then covers her swimmerets with a sticky substance she makes inside her body. Next, she flips onto her back and begins laying her eggs. As the female lays her eggs, the eggs come into contact with the male crayfish's sperm. The sperm fertilizes them. The fertilized eggs become stuck to the female's swimmerets. She sweeps away the eggs that have not been fertilized.

This female crayfish is laying eggs.

Crayfish shelters

Most crayfish make shelters by digging tunnels or holes in soil or sand. The shelters are called **burrows**.

Burrowing down

Crayfish use burrows to stay cool in summer and warm in winter. They often dig burrows on the shores of ponds and other bodies of water. Some crayfish burrows are three feet (1 m) deep. Other crayfish may dig burrows that are up to 30 feet (9 m) deep!

Digging deep

Crayfish dig burrows deep enough to reach **ground water**. Ground water is found under the ground. Ground water seeps up through soil into the bottom of the burrows.

Safe places

Crayfish use their burrows as hiding places. Many crayfish molt in their burrows, where they are safe from predators while they cannot move. Female crayfish cannot move quickly to escape from predators when they have instars attached to their bodies. The females often stay hidden in their burrows until all the instars have left.

This crayfish is coming out of its burrow.

Breathing in burrows

Crayfish do not need to be under water to breathe. They can breathe as long as their gills are moist. Crayfish use the ground water in their burrows to keep their gills moist.

Land ho!

Some crayfish do not live in water. They make burrows and search for food on land. Many land crayfish live in wet soil near water. Some live in soggy fields. A few species of crayfish live in damp caves.

Chimneys

When a crayfish digs a burrow, the dirt from the burrow piles up around the burrow's opening. The dirt pile forms a wall, called a **chimney**, around the burrow. A chimney may be just one inch (2.5 cm) high or up to sixteen inches (41 cm) high.

This Florida cave crayfish is blind. It lives in a dark cave, so it does not need to see.

Dinnertime!

Most crayfish are **nocturnal**. Animals that are nocturnal are active mainly at night. Crayfish use their antennae to search for food at night. They look for food around rocks and logs. A few species of crayfish live in clear water. To look for food, they use their eyes more than they use their antennae. These crayfish often search for food in daylight, when it is bright enough for them to see.

Not fussy eaters

Crayfish are **omnivores**. Omnivores are animals that eat both plants and animals. Crayfish eat many foods, including underwater plants, fish eggs, snails, worms, insects, and even other crayfish! Crayfish are also **scavengers**, or animals that eat dead plants and animals. They even eat rotting plants and animal waste!

This crayfish has found a dead crayfish to eat.

Predators and defenses

Many animals eat crayfish. Birds, alligators, fish, raccoons, snakes, frogs, and mink are all crayfish predators. Crayfish have ways of avoiding and escaping from these animals.

Blending in

Some crayfish have bodies that are **camouflaged**. Crayfish with camouflage have colors, patterns, or textures on their exoskeletons that hide the crayfish in their habitats. It is hard for predators to see camouflaged crayfish.

Quick escapes

A crayfish backs into its burrow so it can see nearby predators. If a predator comes too close, the crayfish hurries away or climbs further into its burrow.

This crayfish was not able to escape from the mink.

Break a leg!

A predator that catches a crayfish by a leg or an antenna may be in for a surprise! The crayfish can flex a muscle and release the body part from the its body! While the predator is left holding the body part, the crayfish quickly escapes. Later, the crayfish grows a new part to replace the part it lost.

Fighting back

A crayfish that has been cornered by a predator can stretch out its body and thrash its legs to make itself appear larger. It can also open and close its claws to warn the predator to leave it alone. In a fight, the crayfish uses its claws to pinch an attacker's body.

Some crayfish, such as this Murray River crayfish, have sharp spines on their exoskeletons. The spines prick predators that bite the crayfish.

Crayfish in danger

The number of Shasta crayfish has dropped so low that they are now endangered.

About 150 species of crayfish are known to be **endangered** or **vulnerable**. An endangered animal is in danger of dying out in the natural place where it lives. An animal that is vulnerable faces threats in its habitat that may cause it to become endangered. Without help, endangered animals may become **extinct**. Extinct animals no longer exist anywhere on Earth.

Human activities

Many human activities put crayfish and other animals in danger. When people **develop** the natural areas in which crayfish live, crayfish lose their habitats. People who live near crayfish habitats often pollute the habitats by using chemicals. The chemicals that people use on lawns run into the water in crayfish habitats when it rains. Crayfish become ill or die in polluted habitats.

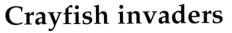

Crayfish invaders

A major problem that crayfish face is the **introduced species** of other crayfish. Introduced species are put into habitats where they do not naturally live. For example, many North American crayfish are raised for food on farms in Asia. These introduced crayfish often escape from the farms. They may carry diseases that can kill the **native species** of crayfish in Asia. Native species are species that naturally live in a habitat. Crayfish are also introduced into habitats when people buy them as pets and then release them into the **wild**.

Many European crayfish die after coming into contact with introduced signal crayfish, such as this one. Signal crayfish were introduced into European habitats from the United States.

Natural disasters

When a **natural disaster** occurs in an area, crayfish are among the many animals that are affected. Violent storms and **droughts**, or long periods without rain, can destroy the plants and animals that crayfish need to survive.

Hurricanes can cause large numbers of crayfish to die.

Helping crayfish

At least half of all known crayfish species need **conservation**. Conservation is protecting habitats and the species that live in them. Crayfish need protection because their **populations** are very small. A population is the total number of one species living in an area. The careless actions of just a few people can quickly wipe out a population of crayfish. Tell your family and friends how important it is to protect crayfish and their habitats!

Get involved

If you are interested in helping crayfish, consider organizing a cleanup of a local freshwater habitat, such as a pond or a stream. Be careful to avoid damaging any crayfish burrows that you find. If you are lucky, you may spot a crayfish around its home! Take notes or draw a picture to help you identify which species you have found.

Show your support

You can also help crayfish and other animals by supporting a local **conservation group**. Conservation groups work to stop **habitat loss** and to protect animals from becoming extinct. They also encourage people to take care of the places that humans and animals share. Contact a conservation group to find out how you can help!

These researchers are looking for introduced signal crayfish. They will remove the signal crayfish from this habitat.

Pet care

If you have a pet crayfish at home or at school, make sure that it lives in a large aquarium with plenty of healthy food. Be careful when handling a pet crayfish—it may try to pinch you with its claws! Never release a store-bought crayfish, such as the one shown right, into the wild. It may cause harm to native crayfish.

Glossary

Note: Boldfaced words that are defined in the text may not appear in the glossary.

compound eye An eye that is made up of many small parts

continent One of the seven large areas of land on Earth (Africa, Antarctica, Asia, Australia, Europe, North America, and South America)

develop To remove plants from an area in order to put up buildings

energy The power that living things need to grow and to move

fertilize To cause an embryo to begin growing

groom To clean and look after eggs

habitat loss The destruction of the natural places where animals live

multicolored Describing something that has many colors

natural disaster A natural event, such as a storm or an earthquake, which causes a lot of damage

nutrients Substances that provide animals with energy

organs Body parts, such as the heart and brain, which do important jobs

wild Describing a place in nature that is not controlled by people

Index

Printed in the U.S.A.